THE COMPLETE LOVE POEMS
OF MAY SWENSON

ALSO BY MAY SWENSON

Another Animal   (1954)

A Cage of Spines   (1958)

To Mix with Time   (1963)

Poems to Solve   (1966)

Half Sun Half Sleep   (1967)

Iconographs   (1970)

More Poems to Solve   (1971)

Windows and Stones   (1972)
(translated from Tomas Tranströmer)

The Guess and Spell Coloring Book   (1976)

New and Selected Things Taking Place   (1978)

In Other Words   (1987)

Nature   (1994)

THE
COMPLETE
LOVE
POEMS
OF
MAY
SWENSON

A MARINER BOOK
Houghton Mifflin Company
BOSTON   NEW YORK   2003

FIRST MARINER BOOKS EDITION 2003

For information about permission to reproduce selections from
this book, write to Permissions, Houghton Mifflin Company,
215 Park Avenue South, New York, New York 10003.

Visit our Web site: www.houghtonmifflinbooks.com.

Library of Congress Cataloging-in-Publication Data is available.
ISBN 0–618–34084-x (pbk.)

Book design by Anne Chalmers
Typefaces: Trump Medieval, Bernhard Modern

Printed in the United States of America

QUM 10 9 8 7 6 5 4 3 2 1

A NUMBER OF POEMS PREVIOUSLY APPEARED IN THE FOLLOW-
ING PUBLICATIONS: *American Poetry Review:* "The Kiss"; *American
Voice:* "The Lone Pedestrian"; *Counter Measures:* "Evening Wind"; *Dallas
Times:* "Equilibrist"; *Formalist:* "To F."; *Kenyon Review:* "Standing Torso";
Ms.: "Good Things Come from Thee" and "In Love Made Visible"; *The Na-
tion:* "Horse" and "Not the Dress"; *New Orlando:* "Who Are You I Saw
Running?"; *Poetry:* "Under the Best of Circumstances"; Paris Review: "Daf-
fodildo"; *Wisconsin Review:* "Cat And I"; *Yale Review:* "The Winepress."
    "Each Day of Summer," "August Night," "A History of Love," "Se-
cure," and "The Tiger's Ghost" are from *Another Animal* by May Swenson.
"A Trellis for R." is reprinted from *Iconographs* by May Swenson. "Little
Lion Face," "Birthday Bush," and "Strawberrying" previously appeared in *In
Other Words* by May Swenson. "Facing," "Our Forward Shadows," "A His-
tory of Love," "You Are," "Wild Water," "Stone or Flame," "The Indivisible
Incompatibles," "Dreams and Ashes," "Night Before the Journey," "Sym-
metrical Companion," "Annual," "Neither Wanting More," and "Because I
Don't Know" were first published in *The Love Poems of May Swenson.* "At
First, at Last," "Beast," "Bleeding," "Digging in the Garden of Age I Uncover
a Live Root," "Goodnight," "Incantation," "Laocoön Dream Recorded in
Diary Dated 1943," "The Little Rapids," "Love Sleeping," "A New Pair," "A
Pair," "The Red Bird Tapestry," "Sketch for a Landscape," and "Zambesi
and Ranee" were first published in *Nature* by May Swenson. "One Morning
in New Hampshire," "A Loaf of Time," "Café Tableau," "Another Animal,"
"Love Is," and "Fireflies" appeared in *To Mix with Time* by May Swenson.
"Somebody" appeared in *Dear Elizabeth* by May Swenson.
    "The Rest of My Life" and "Sleeping with Boa" appeared in *May Swen-
son: A Poet's Life in Photos* by R. R. Knudson and Suzzanne Bigelow.
    The following poems are published for the first time: "Asleep," "Coda to
J.," "Found in a Diary Dated May 29, 1973," "Plea for Delicacy in Love,"
"This Is What My Love Is Thinking," "To a Dark Girl," and "We Arise from
the Pit of Night."

CONTENTS

FOREWORD

WITH RARE EXCEPTION, May Swenson's remarkable love poems, spanning more than five decades, are not gender-specific. Many are cast in big-cat roles involving tigers, lions, jaguars, and other shaggy jungle beasts. Others admire or even take the part of circus artists balancing on tightropes.

In "Symmetrical Companion," the lovers "shall be two daring acrobats/above the staring faces/framed in wheels of light/ visible to millions . . . We shall not fall/as long as our gaze is not severed."

"Unloosed, unharnessed, turned back to the wild by love," Swenson writes in "The School of Desire," "Our discipline was mutual and the art/that spun our dual beauty. While you wheeled/in flawless stride apart,/I, in glittering boots to the fulcrum heeled,/ need hardly signal."

Other poems recreate centaurs in similar cadence, and one imagines Laocoön lovingly held fast by the serpent's coils. Titled "Laocoön Dream Recorded in Diary Dated 1943," the poet details the seven "arms" encircling her in erotic images. "An odd thrill made a geyser in my blood," she writes, after "an arm . . ./but longer than an arm . . . lapped me twice/. . . One supple coil lay nice about my waist/. . . the other . . . slipped/to my hip . . . This love had a new taste."

But setting these role-playing poems aside, the majority of Swenson's love poems are human you-and-I poems, or we poems, exquisitely tender and understated, as in "Holding the Towel," when the poet, on shore, begins to panic: "My squint/lost you to nibbling/waves." When her lover surfaces, her relief is enormous, but all she permits herself is: "I was still/scanning the nearby/nowhere-going boats."

In "In the Yard," the freight of the poem is pulled by the quirky, apt, almost brusque imagery of birds Swenson observes as she awaits her lover's return. The woodpecker: "Redheaded's riddling the phone pole." The oriole: "cheddar under black bold head." The pheasant: "the ringneck who/noseblows twice parades his mate." And then, casually, "You're back barefoot brought some fruit./Split me an apple. We'll get red//white halves each our/juice on the Indian spread." As is often true in poetry, less is more. Much is withheld for the good of the poem.

And what a sure voice Swenson has, whether with the looks and sounds of birds or bees, as in "A Couple": "A bee/rolls/in the yellow/rose./Does she/invite his hairy/rub?//He scrubs/ himself/in her creamy/folds;/a bullet, soft, imposes/her spiral and, spinning, burrows/to her dewy/shadows." Equally deft, an artlessly simple yet equally erotic poem about a dandelion— "Little lion face/. . . streaked flanges of your silk/sunwheel relaxed in wide/dilation"—broadens to these images: "You're/ twisted shut as a burr,/neck drooped unconscious,//an inert, limp bundle,/a furled cocoon . . . Oh, lift your young neck,/ open and expand to your//lover, hot light."

These truncated quotations cannot begin to reproduce the music Swenson creates with the resources of prosody. She is inventive but always linguistically accurate: "Shall we live like the lizard/in the frost of denial?" she asks alliteratively. Elsewhere, she employs assonance ("I gloated on the palomino of your flanks") and personification ("hidden in the hair/the spiral Ear/waits to Suck sound//and sly beneath its/ledge the Eye to Spear/the fish of light").

In 1970 May Swenson published a collection of so-called concrete poems—poems placed on the page to form shapes— that she titled "Iconographs." She seemed to hunger for a new symbiosis that went beyond the format of line and stanza, and she found it in these experimental, idiosyncratic structures. It was her ambition, she explains in a note to that book, "to cause an instant eye-to-eye encounter with each poem even before it is read word-after-word."

Two of her most successful concrete poems, "Bleeding" and "A Trellis for R.," are included in this collection. The first of these is often reprinted because of its inviting shape. It is set typographically so that a jagged cut runs vertically down the page. The two speakers, knife and cut, parry back and forth in a perplexing dialogue which ends: "I feel I have to bleed to feel I think said the cut./I don't I don't have to feel said the knife drying now becoming shiny." Is the poet's intent philosophical rather than sexual? Perhaps. Or is this an emotional, even sadomasochistic dialogue between lovers?

"A Trellis for R.," daring in its time, is Swenson's most overtly sexual poem. It is driven by the design of a lattice for roses she has established on the page, one which is difficult to reproduce in this foreword. But consider these images: "Pink lips the serrate/folds taste smooth/and Rosehip round the center/bud I suck. I milknip//your two Blue/skeined blown Rose/beauties too to sniff their/berries' blood up stiff pink tips."

Lesbian poetry is now so much a part of our culture as to be taken for granted. Excepting the poem just cited, think of the lengths to which Swenson went to preserve her secret "love that dares not speak its name" from a hostile world. And even after the social acceptance of homosexuality, Swenson, like her friend Elizabeth Bishop, maintained her distance from woman-identified poetry.

Still, poems encrypted for safety's sake, as in "Poet to Tiger," come down to us now with a resilience and charm they might not otherwise have had. "Come breathe on me rough pard/put soft paws here," the poet entreats. "Tiger don't scold me/don't make me comb my hair outdoors.//Cuff me careful. Lick don't/crunch. Make last what's yours."

Perhaps without knowing, in "Found in Diary Dated May 29, 1973," Swenson sums up for us the power and pleasure of her work: "Most of what is happening is hidden./There is a sub-world/where the roots of things exist."

— MAXINE KUMIN

THE COMPLETE LOVE POEMS
OF MAY SWENSON

Your eyes are just
like bees, and I
feel like a flower.
Their brown power makes
a breeze go over
my skin. When your
lashes ride down and
rise like brown bees'
legs, your pronged gaze
makes my eyes gauze.
I wish we were
in some shade and
no swarm of other
eyes to know that
I'm a flower breathing
bare, laid open to
your bees' warm stare.
I'd let you wade
in me and seize
with your eager brown
bees' power a sweet
glistening at my core.

MORNINGS INNOCENT

I wear your smile upon my lips
arising on mornings innocent
Your laughter overflows my throat
Your skin is a fleece about me
With your princely walk I salute the sun
People say I am handsome

Arising on mornings innocent
birds make the sound of kisses
Leaves flicker light and dark like eyes

I melt beneath the magnet of your gaze
Your husky breath insinuates my ear
Alert and fresh as grass I wake

and rise on mornings innocent
The strands of the wrestler
run golden through my limbs
I cleave the air with insolent ease
With your princely walk I salute the sun
People say I am handsome

SWIMMERS

Tossed
by the muscular sea,
we are lost,
and glad to be lost
in troughs of rough

love. A bath in
laughter, our dive
into foam,
our upslide and float
on the surf of desire.

But sucked to the root
of the water-mountain —
immense —
about to tip upon us
the terror of total

delight —
we are towed,
helpless in its
swell, by hooks
of our hair;

then dangled, let go,
made to race —
as the wrestling chest
of the sea, itself
tangled, tumbles

in its own embrace.
Our limbs like eels
are water-boned,
our faces lost
to difference and

contour, as the lapping
crests.
They cease
their charge,
and rock us

in repeating hammocks
of the releasing
tide —
until supine we glide,
on cool green

smiles
of an exhaling
gladiator,
to the shore
of sleep.

We wake to double blue:
an ocean without sail,
sky without a clue
of white.
Morning is a veil
sewn of only two
threads, one pale,
one bright.

We bathe as if in ink,
but peacock-eyed and clear;
a roof of periwink
goes steep
into a bell of air
vacant to the brink.
Far as we can peer
is deep

royal blue and shy
iris, queen and king
colors of low
and high.
Then dips
a sickle wing,
we hear a hinged cry:
taut as from a sling

downwhips
a taunting gull.
And now across our gaze
a snowy hull
appears;
triangles
along its stays
break out to windpulls.

With creaking shears
the bright
gulls cut the veil
in two,
and many a clue
on scalloped sail
dots with white
our double blue.

We go to gather berries of rain
(sharp to the eye as ripe to the tongue)
that cluster the woods and, low down
between rough-furrowed pine
trunks, melons of sunlight. Morning, young,
carries a harvest in its horn:
colors, shapes, odors, tones
(various as senses are keen).
High in a grape-transparent fan
of boughs are cones
of crystal that were wooden brown.

Two by two, into our ears
are fed sweet pips from a phoebe's throat,
and buzzy notes from a warbler pair,
nuts chuckled from the score
of the thrasher. Gauzing afloat,
a giant moth comes to the choir,
and hums while he sips
from spangles of fern. Insects whir
like wheat in a circular
bin of light; we hear skip
the husking chipmunks in their lair.

Goblin pears, or apples, or quaint
eggs, the mushrooms
litter the forest loft
on pungent mats, in shade still wet,
the gray of gunny in the gloom —
in sun, bright sawdust.
Here's a crop for the nose:
(relish to sight as motley to scent):
fume of cobwebbed stumps, musky roots,
resin-tincture, bark-balm, dayspring moss
in stars new-pricked (vivid as soft).

Day heats and mellows. Those winking seeds —
or berries — spill from their pods; the path's dry
from noon wood to meadow. A speckled
butterfly on top of a weed is a red
and yellow bloom: if that two-ply
petal could be touched,
or the violet wing of the mountain!
Both out of reach — too wary,
or too far to stroke, unless with the eye.
But in green silk of the rye
grain our whole bodies are cuddled.

In the sun's heart we are ripe
as fruits ourselves, enjoyed
by lips of wind our burnished slopes.
All round us dark, rapt
humble-eyes of susans are deployed
as if to suck our honey-hides. Ants nip,
tasting us all over
with tickling pincers. We are a landscape
to daddy-long-legs, whose ovoid
hub on stilts climbs us like a lover,
trying our dazzle, our warm sap.

EACH DAY OF SUMMER

In the unassembled puzzle of the city
a lava forest ragged crags of roofs
to a ledge hung in rare green
and a narrow garden
in immutable rock a fissure
of living grass
the sun came like a king
each day of summer
with great golden hands
caressed our skin to jasper

Miraculous as if a mounted knight
crowned caparisoned crossed a soot-grim moat
to a round tower ribbon-tipped
each day of summer
love came bearing love
a chalice of light
We bathed in love and drank it
Then our flesh
seemed like the leaves
enameled bright forever

Now the roofs are white with winter's order
the city's million gashes bandaged clean
earth and sinuous tree
stern brick and cobble
by ethereal snow composed to unity
The ledge where the sun
a coat of mail lay on us
now a coffer loaded with pearls of frost
the opulent plume in warm blue
that waved above us
now stark as ivory canopied in gray

But the honey in our veins burned deep
We are stored with sweetness
Our breasts are golden hives
In interior bone
the scepter's knob hoards ruby like a coal
In the eternal sky of mind
each day of summer
paints a lozenge in the prism of our love

A loaf of time
round and thick
So many layers
ledges to climb
to lie on our
bellies lolling
licking our lips
The long gaze a
gull falling
down the cliff's
table   to coast
the constant
waves   The reach-
ing wave-tongues
lick the table
But slowly grayly
slow as the ocean
is gray beyond
the green   slow
as the sky is high
and out of sight
higher than blue
is white   Around
the table's wheel
unbounded   for
each a meal the
centered mound to
be divided   A
wedge for each
and leisure on
each ledge   The
round loaf thick
we lick our lips
Our eyes gull

            down the layered
            cliff and ride
          the reaching waves
      that lick but   slowly
                  the table's
        edge   Then slowly
          our loaf   Slowly
              our ledge

IN THE YARD

Dogwood's s n o w. Its ground's air.
R e d h e a d e d's riddling the phone pole.

Fat-tailed she-dog grinning's
t h r a s h e r - r e d.

It's the oriole there by the feeder
c h e d d a r under b l a c k bold head.

Neighbor doing yardwork's getting r e d.
Lifts tiles to a barrow.

L.I.R.R.'s four cars rollskate by
w h i t e potato blooms farside the field.

That square's our bedroom window.
You're not there. You're away

looking for nails or such
to put up a mirror frame the Adam

and Eve bright hair held back by a
r o b i n's - e g g - b l u e band.

Or you're at the body shop about
the broken bumper.

C a b b a g e b u t t e r f l y's found
h o n e y he thinks on r i n g

g l i n t s on my hand. I wait
for the r i n g n e c k who

noseblows twice parades his mate. She's g r a y.
Until comes the B l u e Bug crunching driveway.

You're back barefoot brought some fruit.
Split me a n a p p l e. We'll get r e d

w h i t e halves each our
juice on the Indian spread.

A bee
rolls
in the yellow
rose.
Does she
invite his hairy
rub?

He scrubs
himself
in her creamy
folds;
a bullet, soft, imposes
her spiral and, spinning, burrows
to her dewy
shadows.

The gold
grooves almost
match
the yellow
bowl.
Does his touch
please
or scratch?

When he's
done
his honey-
thieving
at her matrix,
whirs free
leaving,
she

closes,
still
tall, chill,
unrumpled on her stem.

CAFÉ TABLEAU

Hand of the copper boy
pours tea   deft wrist square fist
salmon-satin-lined

Dark-muscled dancers among porcelain
twined   his fingers and long thumb

He stands dumb in crisp white coat
his blood in heavy neck-vein
eloquent   its flood plunges
to each purple nail   emanates
male electrons

His pupils conscienceless as midnight skies
between the moon-whites of his eyes   avoid
tea-sipper's naked shoulder
diamond-cold her throat

That she is female his broad nostrils
have denied   like figs dried when green
her breasts shrivel in the refusal
of his stare

His thigh athletic slender   retreats
behind her chair   in his hips
nothing tender   ancestral savagery
has left him lion-clean

Furtive beneath mental hedges
she sees   feels his bare wrist square fist
her boneless hand creeps up the crisp sleeve
higher   she squeals and finds the nipples
of his hairless chest

The copper boy's white coat
becomes a loincloth she unwinds   he wades
into the pool of her stagnant desire

all we see as yet
slant tall
and timid
on the floor

the stage is set
each waits
in the long-lit door

a bell in the wings
far in the painted forest
rings announcing delight

ourselves
still out of sight
our shadows listen

the cue
summons the dance
of me and you

advance
where our shadows meet
already loved

invade the room
with the scent
of thunder in the blood

move on the colored flood
naked
needing no costume

we are dressed
each in the other's kisses

our shadows reach
to teach us our parts

the enchanted prelude starts

ORGANS

hidden in the hair
the spiral Ear
waits to Suck sound

and sly beneath its
ledge the Eye to Spear
the fish of light

the Mouth's a hole
and yet a Cry for
love for loot

with every stolen
breath the Snoot
Supposes roses

nose tongue fishing
eye's Crouched
in the same hutch

nibbling lips and
funnel's there
in the legs' lair
carnivora of Touch

FACING

1   2

You I love
you are that light
by which I am discovered.
In anonymous night
by your eye am I born.
And I know
that by your body I glow,
and by your face
I make my circle.
It is your heat
fires me
that my skin is sweet
my veins race
my bones are radiant.

You are that central One
by which I am balanced.
By your power it is done
that in the sky of being
my path is thrown.
And I glide in your sling
and cannot fall into darkness.
For by the magnet
of your body
charged with love
do I move.

As you are sun to me
O I am moon to you.
And give you substance
by my sight
and motion and radiance.
You are an ocean
shaped by my gaze.
My pulsing rays
draw you naked
from the spell of night.
By my pull
are you waked
to know that you are beautiful.

I rake up your steep
luster and your passion;
by my sorcery your wealth is sown
to you on your own breast,
your purples changed to opals.

So with love's light
I sculpture you
and in my constant mirror keep
your portrait
that you may adore
yourself as I do.

Two white whales have been installed at
the Waldorf. They are tumbling slowly
above the tables, butting the chandeliers,
submerging, and taking soft bites
out of the red-vested waiters in the
Peacock Room. They are poking *fleur-de-lys*
tails into the long pockets on the
waiters' thighs. They are stealing
breakfast strawberries from two eccentric
guests — one, skunk-cabbage green with
dark peepers — the other, wild rose and
milkweed, barelegged, in Lafayette loafers.
When the two guests enter the elevator,
the whales ascend, bouncing, through all
the ceilings, to the sixth floor. They
get between the sheets. There they turn
candy-pink, with sky-colored eyes, and
silver bubbles start to rise from velvet
navels on the tops of their heads.
Later, a pale blue VW, running on poetry,
weaves down Park Avenue, past yellow
sprouts of forsythia, which, due to dog-do
and dew, are doing nicely. The two
white whales have the blue car in tow
on a swaying chain of bubbles. They are
rising toward the heliport on the Pan Am
roof. There they go, dirigible and slow,
hide-swiping each other, lily tails flipping,
their square velvet snouts stitched with
snug smiles. It is April. "There's
a kind of hush all over the world."

TO F.

The el ploughs down the morning
The newsboys stand in wait
Sunlight lashes the cobbles
We reach the crosstown gate

Your bus will stop at Christopher
Mine at Abingdon Square
Your hand . . . "Good luck" and mine . . . "So long"
The taxi trumpets blare

The green light turns, a whistle blows
Our steps divide the space
Between our day-long destinies
But still I see your face

Whirling through the crowded hours
Down the afternoon
Lurking in my thoughts, your smile
Pricks me like a tune

The acrobat astride his swing in space
the pole rolled under his instep
catches the pits of his knees
is lipped by his triangled groin
fits the fold of his hard-carved buttocks

Long-thighed tight-hipped he drops
head-down and writhes erect
glazed smooth by speed a twirled top
sits immobile in the void

Gravity outwhipped squeezed like dough
is kneaded to his own design
a balance-egg at the plexus of his bowels
counteracting vertigo

Empty of fear and therefore without weight
he walks a wedge of steeper air
indifferent to the enormous stare
of onlookers in rims of awe below

Drums are solid blocks beneath him
Strong brass horn-tones prolong him
on glittering stilts

Self-hurled he swims the color-stippled height
where nothing but whisks of light
can reach him

At night he is my lover

AUGUST NIGHT

Shadow like a liquid lies
   in your body's hollows
In your eyes garnet stars
   shift their facets with your breath
The August night is Nubian
   something green mixed with the dark
a powder for your skin that tints
   the implications of your bones
with copper light
   an aura round your knees your navel
a little pool with pulsing tide

Is there beauty deeper than your cool
   form drawn by the occult stylus
of this night
   slanting to autumn
the long dawn soon bringing wrappings
   for your breast?
Has any other watchman stiller stayed
   to the smiting of this gong
half in glory half afraid to look
   at what obscure in light
is now explained by shade?

FIREFLIES

Fireflies throw
love winks
to their kind
on the dark, glow
without heat,

their day bodies
common beetles.
In a planetarium
of the mind
sparks lit

when logic has gone
down
faint in the dawn
of intellect.
Instinct

makes luminous
the insect.
Idea's anonymous
ordinary mark,
that cryptic

in daylight crept,
can rise an asterisk
astonishing others out.
If the secret
of the dark

be kept,
an eagerness
in smallest, fiercest
hints
can scintillate.

In love are we made visible
As in a magic bath
are unpeeled
to the sharp pit
so long concealed

With love's alertness
we recognize
the soundless whimper
of the soul
behind the eyes
A shaft opens
and the timid thing
at last leaps to surface
with full-spread wing

The fingertips of love discover
more than the body's smoothness
They uncover a hidden conduit
for the transfusion
of empathies that circumvent
the mind's intrusion

In love are we set free
Objective bone
and flesh no longer insulate us
to ourselves alone
We are released
and flow into each other's cup
Our two frail vials pierced
drink each other up

Passing a lank boy, bangs to the eyebrows,
licking a Snow Flake cone, and cones on the tulip tree
   up stiff, honeysuckle tubelets weighting a vine,
and passing *Irene Gay — Realtor, The Black Whale, Rexall,*
   and others — (Irene, don't sue me, it's just your sign
I need in the scene) —
   remembering lilac a month back, a different faded shade,
buying a paper with the tide table instead of the twister
   forecast on page three,
then walking home from the village, beneath the viaduct,
   I find Midwest echoes answering echoes
that another, yet the same train, wakes here out East.
   I'm thinking of how I leaned on you, you leaning
in the stone underpass striped with shadows of tracks
   and ties, and I said, "Give me a kiss, A.D.,
even if you are tranquilized," and I'm thinking
   of the Day of the Kingfisher, the Indigo Day of the Bunting,
of the Catfish Night I locked the keys in the car
   and you tried to jimmy in, but couldn't, with a clothes hanger.
The night of the juke at Al's — *When Something's Wrong*
   With My Baby — you pretended to flake out on the bench,
and I poured icy Scotch into the thimble of your belly,
   lifting the T-shirt. Another night you threw up
in a Negro's shoe. It's Accabonac now instead of
   Tippecanoe. I'm remembering how we used to drive
to *The Custard* "to check out the teenage boxes."
   I liked the ones around the Hondas, who
from a surly distance, from under the hair in their eyes,
   cruised the girls in flowered shorts.
One day back there, licking cones, we looked in
   on a lioness lying with her turd behind the gritty window
of a little zoo. I liked it there. I'd like it
   anywhere with you.
Here there are gorgeous pheasants, no hogs, blond horses,

and Alec Guinness seen at *The Maidstone* Memorial Eve —
and also better dumps. You scavenged my plywood desk top,
    a narrow paint-flecked old door, and the broad white
wicker I'm sitting in now.
    While you're at the dump hunting for more —
maybe a double spring good as that single you climbed to
    last night (and last year) — I sit in front of a house,
remembering a house back there, thinking of a house —
    where? when? — by spring next year?
I notice the immature oak leaves, vivid as redbud almost,
    and shaped like the spoor of the weasel we saw
once by the Wabash.
    Instead of "to the *Readmore*" riffling *Playboy*, I found
you yesterday in that Newtown Lane newspaper store
    I don't yet know the name of. Stay with me, A.D.,
don't blow. Scout out that bed. Go find tennis
    instead of squash mates, surfboarders, volleyball
boys to play with. I know you will, before long —
    maybe among the lifeguards — big, cool-coned,
straight-hipped, stander-on-one-finger, strong.

Unloosed, unharnessed, turned back to the wild by love,
the ring you cantered round with forelock curled,
the geometric music of this world
dissolved and, in its place,
alien as snow to tropic tigers, amphitheatric space,
you will know the desert's freedom, wind and sun
rough-currying your mane, the plenitude
of strong caresses on your body nude.

Released to run from me. Then will I stand
alone in the hoof-torn ring,
lax in my hand
as wine leaked out the thin whip of my will,
and gone the lightning-string
between your eye and mine.

Our discipline was mutual and the art
that spun our dual beauty. While you wheeled
in flawless stride apart,
I, in glittering boots to the fulcrum heeled,
need hardly signal: your prideful head
plunged to the goad of love-looks sharper than ice.

I gloated on the palomino of your flanks, the nice
sprightliness of pace,
your posture like Apollo's steed. I stood my place
as in a chariot,
held the thong of studded light, the lariat
that made you halt, or longer leap, or faster.
But you have bridled me, bright master.

On wild, untrampled slopes you will be monarch soon,
and I the mount that carries you to those high

prairies steeped in noon.
In the arena where your passion will be spent
in loops of speed, sky's indigo unbounded
by the trainer's tent,
instead of oboes, thunder's riddle,
rain for the racing fifes, I will be absent.

When orchestras of air shall vault you
to such freedom, joy and power,
I will cut the whip that sent you there, will put
away the broken ring, and shut
the school of my desire.

The Hair

You went downstairs
saw a hair in the sink
and squeezed my toothpaste by the neck.
You roared. My ribs are sore.
This morning even my pencil's got your toothmarks.
Big Cat Eye cocked on me you see bird bones.
Snuggled in the rug of your belly
your breath so warm
I smell delicious fear.
Come breathe on me rough pard
put soft paws here.

The Salt

You don't put salt on anything
so I'm eating without.
Honey on the eggs is all right
mustard on the toast.
I'm not complaining I'm saying I'm
living with *you*.
You like your meat raw
don't care if it's cold.
Your stomach must have tastebuds
you swallow so fast.
Night falls early. It's foggy. Just now

I found another of your bite marks in the cheese.
I'm hungry. Please
come bounding home
I'll hand you the wine to open
with your teeth.
Scorch me a steak unsalted
boil my coffee twice

say the blessing to a jingle on the blue TV.
Under the lap robe on our chilly couch
look behind my ears "for welps"
and hug me.

The Sand

You're right I brought a grain
or two of sand
into bed I guess in my socks.
But it was you pushed them off
along with everything else.

Asleep you flip
over roll
everything under
you and off
me. I'm always grabbing
for my share of the sheets.

Or else you wake me every hour with sudden
growled I-love-yous
trapping my face between those plushy
shoulders. All my float-dreams turn spins
and never finish. I'm thinner
now. My watch keeps running fast.
But best is when we're riding pillion
my hips within your lap. You let me steer.
Your hand and arm go clear
around my ribs your moist
dream teeth fastened on my nape.

A grain of sand in the bed upsets you or
a hair on the floor.
But you'll get

in slick and wet from the shower if I let
you. Or with your wool cap
and skiing jacket on
if it's cold.
Tiger don't scold me
don't make me comb my hair outdoors.

Cuff me careful. Lick don't
crunch. Make last what's yours.

The Dream

You get into the tub holding *The Naked Ape*
in your teeth. You wet that blond
three-cornered pelt lie back wide
chest afloat. You're reading
in the rising steam and I'm
drinking coffee from your tiger cup.
You say you dreamed
I had your baby book
and it was pink and blue.
I pointed to a page and there
was your face with a cub grin.

You put your paws in your armpits
make a tiger-moo.
Then you say: "Come here
Poet and take
this hair
off me." I do.
It's one of mine. I carefully
kill it and carry
it outside. And stamp on it
and bury it.

In the begonia bed.
And then take off my shoes
not to bring a grain
of sand in to get
into our bed.
I'm going to
do the cooking
now instead
of you.
And sneak some salt in
when you're not looking.

Other than self
O inconceivable
How touched how kissed?
There was a lodestone
made the stars rush down
like pins that fastened us together
under the same dark cloak
We were stroked
by some magician's fur

Each became a doll
Our pure amazement
bestowed us perfect gifts
Our cravings were surpassed
by the porcelain eyes
alluring lips caressable hair
Undressed we handled ivory idols

Summer winter fall and still delighted
unmarred in the dangerous game of change
Replaced by the wonder of the found
the so long kept
The dear endurable surprised us more
than the ecstasies of ritual spring
Like Nature her transfers we adored our everydays
the never knowing what
next the sprites within us would disclose

At last acquainted smoothed by contiguity
sharpened each by opposite tempers we divined
about our nacreous effigies outlined
the soft and mortal other
Under the body's plush a density
awkward ambiguous as bone
Real as our own

O other than self
and O believable
The dream tent fallen
daylight come
we wake to a nakedness so actual
our magnet a common innocent stone

Else than beauty
else than passion then?
Their amalgam mingled mounted up to this
How sweet the plain
how warm the true
We by this mystery charmed anew
begin again to love

ANOTHER ANIMAL

Another animal imagine moving
  in his rippling hide
    down the track of the centaur
      Robust inside him his heart siphons unction to his muscles
        proving
          this columnar landscape lives
            Last night's dream
              flinches at the mind's lattice
              transformed into a seam of sunlight on his trunk
            that like a tree
          shimmers in ribbons of shadow
        His mystery the invert cloud engulfs me with the grass

    Imagine another moving
  even as I pass
among the trees that need not shift their feet
  to pierce the sky's academy
    and let go their leaves
      let go
        their leaves
          bright desperate as cries
            and do not cry
              Even as I he breathes
                and shall be breathless
              for the mind-connected pulse
            heaves hurries halts for but two reasons
          Loveless then deathless
        but if loved
      surrendered to the season's summit
    the ice-hood the volcano's hiccough
  the empty-orbed zero of eclipse

The lean track dips together where our feet have pounced
   The rugs the pine boughs gave us glisten clean
     We meet like two whelps at their mother's dugs
      Does the earth trounced here recall
        the hipmarks of another fall
           when dappled animals with hooves and human knees
            coupled in the face of the convulsive spurning
          of other cities and societies?

      We are wizards mete for burning
    and rush forward to our fate
    neighing as when centaurs mate

    Unable to imagine until late
  in the September wood
that another stood out of God's pocket
   straddled between beast and human
     now each the other's first stern teacher
      learns the A and B against the bitten lips
       Our coiled tongues strike the first word
      Turned heels our star-crossed hands
        kick the mind to its ditch in leaf-mold
          Open to joy to punishment in equal part
         closed to the next mutation
           we lie locked at the forking of the heart

SECURE

Let us deceive ourselves a little
while   Let us pretend that air
is earth   and falling lie resting
within each other's gaze   Let us

deny that flame consumes   that
fruit ripens   that the wave must
break   Let us forget the circle's
fixed beginning marks to the
instant its ordained end   Let us

lean upon the moment and expect
time to enfold us   space sustain
our weight   Let us be still   and
falling lie face to face and drink
each other's breath   Be still
Let us be still   We lie secure

within the careful mind of death

you are my mirror
in your eye's well I float
my reality proven

          I dwell
          in you
          and so
          I know
          I am

no one
can be sure
by himself
of his own being

          and the world's seeing
        the fleeting mirrors of others' eyes
        cloudy abstracted remote
        or too bright convex false directly smiling
        or crepuscular under their lids
        crawling the ground like snails
        or narrowed
        nervously hooked to the distance
            is suspect

do I live
does the world live
do I live in it
or does it live in me?

        because you believe I exist I exist
        I exist in your verdant garden
           you have planted me
           I am glad to grow

I dream of your hands by day
all day I dream of evening
when you will open the gate
come out of the noisy world
to tend me

                    to pour at my roots
                    the clear the flashing water
                    of your love
and exclaim over my new leaf
and stroke it with a broad finger
as if a god surprised fondled his first earth-sprig

                    once I thought
                    to seek the limits
                    of all being
          I believed
          in my own eyes' seeing
          then
                    to find pattern purpose aim
                    thus forget death
                    or forgive it
then I thought
to plumb the heart of death
to cicatrize that spot
and plot abolishment
          so that pattern shape and purpose
          would not gall me
          I would be its part forever
          content in never falling
          from its web

                    now I know
                    beginning and end
                    are one
                    and slay each other
but their offspring is what *is*
not was or will be

                    am I? yes
                    and never was
                    until you made me
                    crying there you are!
                    and I unfurled in your rich soil
I am the genie
in your eye's well
crouching there
so that you must take me with you everywhere
an underwater plant in a secret cylinder
                              you the vial
                              and I the vine
                              and I twining inside you

and you glad
to hold me
floating there
                    for if I live in you
                    you live holding me
                    enfolding me you *are*
it is proven and the universe exists!
                              one reflects the other
                              man mirrors god
                              image in eye affirms its sight
                              green stem in earth attests
                              its right to spin
                              in palpable roundness

is this then
what is meant
that god is love
and is that all?

how simple and how sure
at the very hub of hazard
so seeming fearful fragile insecure
two threads
in the web of chaos
lashed by the dark daemonic wind
crossed upon each other
therefore fixed and still
axial in the bursting void
are perpetual each according to the other

I am
then I am a garden too
and tend you

        my eye is a mirror
        in which you float
        a well where you dwell smiling

    I the vial
    hold you
    a vine a twining genie
I enfold you
and secrete the liquid
of your being
in that I love you
and you live *in* me

The tiger
and the tiger's passion
haunt this cell
in their own fashion

These cool walls
this empty place
remember well
the tiger's face
remember well
the tiger's yawn
as candle-eyed
he grinned upon
a stain of moonlight
on the floor
cleft by bars

The tiger's roar
consumed this silence
roused this stone
to raucous echo

O alone
the tiger stretched
on velvet flank
lapped by night

This room is rank
with carnal rage
and jungle smell
The tiger's ghost
lurks in this cell

I had a dream in which I had a
dream,
and in my dream I told you,
"Listen, I will tell you my
dream." And I began to tell you. And
you told me, "I haven't time to listen while you tell your
dream."

Then in my dream I
dreamed I began to
forget my
dream.
And I forgot my
dream.
And I began to tell you, "Listen, I have
forgot my
dream."
And now I tell you: "Listen while I tell you my
dream, a
dream
in which I dreamed I
forgot my
dream,"
and I begin to tell you: "In my dream you told me, 'I haven't time to
listen.' "

And you tell me: "You dreamed I wouldn't
listen to a
dream that you
forgot?
I haven't time to listen to
forgotten
dreams."

"But I haven't forgot I
                dreamed," I tell you,
        "a dream in which I told you,
            'Listen, I have
            forgot,' and you told me, 'I haven't time.' "
"I haven't time," you tell me.

And now I begin to forget that I
                forgot what I began to tell you in my
                dream.
        And I tell you, "Listen,
                listen, I begin to
                forget."

Insidious cruelty is this
that will allow the heart
a scent of wild water
in the arid land —
that holds out the cup
but to withdraw the hand.

Then says to the heart: Be glad
that you have beheld the font
where lies requitement,
and identified your thirst.
Now, heart, take up your desert;
this spring is cursed.

Shall we pray to be delivered
from the crying of the flesh
Shall we live like the lizard
in the frost of denial

Or shall we offer the nerve-buds
of our bodies
to be nourished (or consumed)
in the sun of love

Shall we wrap ourselves rigid
against desire's contagion
in sarcophagi of safety
insulate ourselves
from both fire and ice

And will the vessel of the heart
stay warm
if our veins be drained of passion
Will the spirit rise virile
from the crematory ash

Shall we borrow
from the stone
relentless peace
or from the flame
exquisite suicide?

Is there anything I can do
or has everything been done
or do
you prefer somebody else to do
it or don't
you trust me to do
it right or is it hopeless and no one can do
a thing or do
you suppose I don't
really want to do
it and am just saying that or don't
you hear me at all or what?

You're
waiting for
the right person the doctor or
the nurse the father or
the mother or
the person with the name you keep
mumbling in your sleep
that no one ever heard of there's no one
named that really
except yourself maybe

If I knew what your name was I'd
prove it's your
own name spelled backwards or
twisted in some way the one you
keep mumbling but you
won't tell me your
name or
don't you know it
yourself that's it
of course you've

forgotten or
never quite knew it or
weren't willing to believe it

Then there *is* something I
can do I
can find your name for you
that's the key to everything once you'd
repeat it clearly you'd
come awake you'd
get up and walk knowing where you're
going where you
came from

And you'd
love me
after that or would you
hate me?
no once you'd
get there you'd
remember and love me
of course I'd
be gone by then I'd
be far away

One stood still, looking stupid. The other,
beak open, streaming a thin sound,
held wings out, took sideways steps,
stamping the salt marsh. It looked threatening.
The other still stood wooden, a decoy.

He stamp-danced closer, his wings arose,
their hinges straightened,
from the wedge-wide beak the thin sound
streaming agony-high —
in fear she wouldn't stand? She stood.

Her back to him pretended —
was it welcome, or only dazed
admission of their fate?
Lifting, he streamed a warning
from his beak, and lit

upon her, trod upon her
back, both careful feet.
The wings held off his weight.
His tail pressed down, slipped off. She
animated. And both went back to fishing.

You swam out
through the boats
your head an orange

buoy sun-daubed
bobbing. My squint
lost you to nibbling

waves. I looked
for a mast to tilt
to glint with your splash

but couldn't see
past the huddled boats.
I found round heads sun-red

dipping rising tipping.
They were tethered
floats. When you dove

from the stovepipe
buoy in the far
furrow of the channel

I was still
scanning the nearby
nowhere-going boats.

THE INDIVISIBLE INCOMPATIBLES

They are like flame and ice
the elemental You and Me
Will nothing then suffice
but they shall extinguished be?

I am locked in glacial pride
You burn with impetuous scorn
My prison is silence
Your arena is wrath
They are opposed as night and morn

If this is so how can it be
we sought each other long ago
and crept together hungrily?

You are quenched in my cold heart
as I dissolve in your core of fire
Then why do we crave each other's touch
magnetized by one desire?

When one forged his armor so
bright as ice and cold as slate
did he divine a spear so swift
and savage as to penetrate?

When one wrapped himself in flame
and emerged a glowing tool
did he dream of substances
irresistible and cool?

Yes
but in fusion
such raw alloys
instantly each the other destroys

BIRTHDAY BUSH

Our bush bloomed, soon dropped
its fuchsia chalices. Rags
on the ground that were luscious
cups and trumpets, promises and brags.

A sprinkle of dark dots showed entry
into each silk cone. Down among
crisp pistils thirsty bumblebees
probed. Buds flared in a bunch

from tender stems. Sudden
vivid big bouquets
appeared just before our birthdays!
A galaxy our burning bush,

blissful explosion. Brief
effusion. Brief as these
words. I sweep away a trash
of crimson petals.

Little lion face
I stooped to pick
among the mass of thick
succulent blooms, the twice

streaked flanges of your silk
sunwheel relaxed in wide
dilation, I brought inside,
placed in a vase. Milk

of your shaggy stem
sticky on my fingers, and
your barbs hooked to my hand,
sudden stings from them

were sweet. Now I'm bold
to touch your swollen neck,
put careful lips to slick
petals, snuff up gold

pollen in your navel cup.
Still fresh before night
I leave you, dawn's appetite
to renew our glide and suck.

An hour ahead of sun
I come to find you. You're
twisted shut as a burr,
neck drooped unconscious,

an inert, limp bundle,
a furled cocoon, your
sun-streaked aureole
eclipsed and dun.

Strange feral flower asleep
with flame-ruff wilted,
all magic halted,
a drink I pour, steep

in the glass for your
undulant stem to suck.
Oh, lift your young neck,
open and expand to your

lover, hot light.
Gold corona, widen to sky.
I hold you lion in my eye
sunup until night.

We are eager
We pant
We whine like whips cutting the air
The frothing sea
the roaring furnace
the jeweled eyes of animals call to us
and we stand frozen
moving neither forward nor back

In the breathless wedge between night and dawn
when the rill of blood pauses at the sluice of the heart
either to advance or retreat
the stars stare at us face to face
penetrating even the disguise of our nakedness
daring us to make the upward leap
effortless as falling
if only we relax the bowstring of our will

We seek the slippery flesh of other men
expecting to be comforted
or to be punished
or to be delighted beyond imagined delights
to be made clean
or to be baptized in the cool font of evil

We believe in the meeting of lips
in the converging of glances
that a talisman is given
that we shall arise anew
be healed and made whole
or be torn at last from our terrible womb-twin
our very self

We are loved in the image of the dead
We love in the image of the never-born
We shudder to beget with child

We shudder not to beget with child
We scream in the doorway of our beginning
We weep at the exit gate

We are alone and never alone
bound and never secured
let go and never freed
We would dance and are hurled
would build and are consumed
We are dragged backward by the past
jerked forward by the future

Our earth a bloody clot of the sun's cataclysm
sun a severed limb of a shattered universe
In fission
explosion
In separation
congealment

I saw two trees embracing.
One leaned on the other
as if to throw her down.
But she was the upright one.
Since their twin youth, maybe she
had been pulling him toward her
all that time,

and finally almost uprooted him.
He was the thin, dry, insecure one,
the most wind-warped, you could see.
And where their tops tangled
it looked like he was crying
on her shoulder.
On the other hand, maybe he

had been trying to weaken her,
break her, or at least
make her bend
over backwards for him
just a little bit.
And all that time
she was standing up to him

the best she could.
She was the most stubborn,
the straightest one, that's a fact.
But he had been willing
to change himself —
even if it was for the worse —
all that time.

At the top they looked like one
tree, where they were embracing.
It was plain they'd be
always together.
Too late now to part.
When the wind blew, you could hear
them rubbing on each other.

Only on the anvil's edge
where the blue fire flashes
will my lead love turn to gold
The rest is dreams and ashes

Only in sleep or solitude
where fancy's fountain plashes
will my dead love rise to swim
The rest is dreams and ashes

Only on the unmarked page
wherever the bold mind dashes
will my fled love follow me
The rest is dreams and ashes

UNTITLED

I   will   be   earth   you   be   the   flower
You   have   found my   root   you   are   the   rain
I   will   be   boat   and   you   the   rower
You   rock   you   toss   me   you   are   the   sea
How   be   steady earth   that's now   a   flood
The   root's the   oar's   afloat where's blown our   bud
We   will   be   desert pure   salt   the   seed
Burn radiant sex   born   scorpion need

SATANIC FORM

Numerals forkmarks of Satan
Triangles circles squares
hieroglyphs of death
Things invented
abortions smelling of the forge
licked to gruesome smoothness by the lathe
Things metallic or glass
frozen twisted flattened
stretched to agonized bubbles
Bricks beams receptacles vehicles
forced through fire hatched to unwilling form
O blasphemies
Time caught in a metal box
Incongruous the rigid clucking tongue
the needled hands the 12-eyed face
against the open window past which drops the night
like a dark lake on end or flowing hair
Night unanimous over all the city
The knuckled fist of the heart opening and closing
Flower and stone not cursed with symmetry
Cloud and shadow not doomed to shape and fixity
The intricate body of man without rivet or nail
or the terrible skirl of the screw
O these are blessed
Satanic form geometry of death
The lariat around the neck of space
The particles of chaos in the clock
The bottle of the yellow liquor light
that circumvents the sifting down of night
O love the juice in the green stem growing
you cannot synthesize
It corrodes in phials and beakers
evaporates in the hot breath of industry
escapes to the air and the dew
returns to the root of the unborn flower
O Satan cheated of your power

It is the last night of the world.
I am allowed once more to show my love.
I place a jewel on a cushion.
I make a juggler's trick.
I become a graceful beast to play with you.

See here something precious, something dazzling:
A garden to be your home,
vast and with every fruit.
The air of mountains for your garment.
The sun to be your servant.
A magic water for you to bathe in
and step forth immortal.

But it is the last night of the world,
and time itself is dying.
Tomorrow my love, locked in the box of my body,
will be shipped away.

THE SHAPE OF DEATH

What does love look like? We know
the shape of death. Death is a cloud
immense and awesome. At first a lid
is lifted from the eye of light:
There is a clap of sound, a white blossom

belches from the jaw of fright,
a pillared cloud churns from white to gray
like a monstrous brain that bursts and burns,
then turns sickly black, spilling away,
filling the whole sky with ashes of dread;

thickly it wraps, between the clean sea
and the moon, the earth's green head.
Trapped in its cocoon, its choking breath,
we know the shape of death:
Death is a cloud.

What does love look like?
Is it a particle, a star —
invisible entirely, beyond the microscope and Palomar?
A dimension unimagined, past the length of hope?
Is it a climate far and fair that we shall never dare

discover? What is its color, and its alchemy?
Is it a jewel in the earth — can it be dug?
Or dredged from the sea? Can it be bought?
Can it be sown and harvested?
Is it a shy beast to be caught?

Death is a cloud,
immense, a clap of sound.
Love is little and not loud.
It nests within each cell, and it
cannot be split.

It is a ray, a seed, a note, a word,
a secret motion of our air and blood.
It is not alien, it is near —
our very skin —
a sheath to keep us pure of fear.

SYMMETRICAL COMPANION

It must be
there walks somewhere in the world
another
another namely like me

Not twin
but opposite
as my two hands are opposite

Where are you
my symmetrical companion?

Do you inhabit
the featureless fog
of the future?
Are you sprinting
from the shadows of the past
to overtake me?
Or are you camouflaged
in the colored present?
Do I graze you every day
as yet immune to your touch
unaware of your scent
inert under your glance?

Come to me
Whisper your name
I will know you instantly
by a passport
decipherable to ourselves alone

We shall walk uniformed
in our secret
We shall be a single reversible cloak

lined with light within
furred with dark without

Nothing shall be forbidden us
All bars shall fall before us
Even the past shall be lit behind us
and seen to have led
like two predestined corridors
to the vestibule of our meeting

We shall be two daring acrobats
above the staring faces
framed in wheels of light
visible to millions
yet revealed only to each other
in the tiny circular mirrors
of our pupils

We shall climb together
up the frail ladders
balancing on slender
but steel-strong thongs of faith
When you leap
my hands will be surely there
at the arc's limit
We shall synchronize
each step of the dance upon the wire
We shall not fall
as long as our gaze is not severed

Where are you
my symmetrical companion?

Until I find you
my mouth is locked

my heart is numb
my mind unlit
my limbs unjointed

I am a marionette
doubled up in a dark trunk
a dancer frozen
in catatonic sleep
a statue locked
in the stone
a Lazarus wrapped
in the swaddling strips
not of death
but of unborn life

a melody bound
in the strings of the viol
a torrent imprisoned
in ice
a flame buried
in the coal
a jewel hidden
in a block of lava

Come release me
Without you I do not yet exist

EVOLUTION

the stone
would like to be
Alive like me

the rooted tree
longs to be Free

the mute beast
envies my fate
Articulate

on this ball
half dark
half light
i walk Upright
i lie prone
within the night

beautiful each Shape
to see
wonderful each Thing
to name
here a stone
there a tree
here a river
there a Flame

marvelous to Stroke
the patient beasts
within their yoke

how i Yearn
for the lion
in his den
though he spurn
the touch of men

the longing
that i know
is in the Stone also
it must be

the same that rises
in the Tree
the longing
in the Lion's call
speaks for all

oh to Endure
like the stone
sufficient
to itself alone

or Reincarnate
like the tree
be born each spring
to greenery

or like the lion
without law
to roam the Wild
on velvet paw

but if walking
i meet
a Creature like me
on the street
two-legged
with human face
to recognize
is to Embrace

wonders pale
beauties dim
during my delight
with Him

an Evolution strange
two Tongues touch
exchange
a Feast unknown
to stone
or tree or beast

ANNUAL

(A LOVE POEM)

Beginning in the spring again
with eyes as new as leaves,
skin like the fox whose hair
hears what the river says,
nostrils locate the mole,
the turnip, the lowest stone,
tongue tastes moonlight:

beginning in the spring again,
blood wild as wind,
limbs loose as the antelope's,
and brain a basket,
lungs think air, mouth remembers
water and all transparent things:

the youngest nerve and keenest stem,
in secret shade, reach up to meet
radiance, swell to make radiance;
as all pouting blossoms do,
I turn, as earth to its sky, to you:

cave of the day's light smiling
into my throat,
meadow of stars, white
on the loam of my dream,
to your cloud-pure bones
that water my yearnings
beginning in the spring again:

turn to the lightning, your laughter
that suddens me, your hair
a wind that stings me,

your breast a fleece of birds
that hover me,
naked, dawn-colored, cool and warm,

I open to your dew,
beginning in the spring again.

To lie with you
in a field of grass
to lie there forever
and let time pass

Touching lightly
shoulder and thigh
Neither wanting more
Neither asking why

To have your whole
cool body's length
along my own
to know the strength
of a secret tide
of longing seep
into our veins
go deep . . . deep

Dissolving flesh
and melting bone
Oh to lie with you
alone

To feel your breast
rise with my sigh
To hold you mirrored
in my eye

Neither wanting more
Neither asking why

Because I don't know you, I love you:
warm cheeks, full lips, rich smile,
dark irises that slide to the side;
thick lashes, thick hair, gleaming
teeth and eyes; your hand in greeting
warmer than mine, wider, in blue shirt,
rolled sleeves, in dark jeans belted —
I liked your robust shoulders, wide neck and
tipped-up chin. That glow is blood
under skin that's warm to begin with,
almost dusky, the red showing
through — of health, of youth — but more:
your open, welcome, I-could-hug-you look.
We met once or twice, exchanged smiles:
your lips, curl-cornered to my thin,
crooked grin; your easy, laughing eyes
to my sharp stare. Did it pierce you
there, my look of hunger, like a hook?
I wanted only a sniff, a tongue-tip's
taste, a moment's bath in your rare
warmth. That last night, trading
goodbyes, when we kissed — or *you* did, me —
my hand took your nape, plunged under
the thick spill of your hair. Then
I stepped into the dark, out of the light
of the party, the screen door's yellow
square sliding smaller and smaller behind
me. You've become a dream of ripe
raspberries, in summer country: deep, dark
red lips, clean, gleaming generous smile.
Who owns you? I don't know. I'll hide you
away in my dream file. Stay there. Don't
change. I don't know you — and had better
not. Because I don't know you, I love you.

A TRELLIS FOR R.

B
L
U
E but you are R
       o
       s
       e too
and buttermilk but with blood
dots showing through.
A little salty your white

nape boy-wide. Glinting hairs shoot
back of your ears' R
       o
       s
       e that
tongue likes to feel
the maze of slip into
the funnel tell a thunder whisper to.
When I kiss

your eyes' straight lashes
down crisp go like doll's
blond straws. Glazed
iris R
   o
   s
   e
   s your lids unclose
to B
   l
   u
     e ringed targets their dark
sheen spokes almost green. I sink in
B
l
u
e black R
      o
      s
      e heart holes until
you blink.

Pink lips the serrate
folds taste smooth
and R
   o
   s
   e
   h
   i
   p round the center
bud I suck. I milknip

your two B
     l
     u
     e skeined blown R
             o
             s
             e
beauties too to sniff their
berries' blood up stiff pink tips.
You're white

in patches only mostly R
             o
             s
             e
buck skin and salty
speckled like a sky. I
love your spots your white neck R
                  o
                  s
                  e
your hair's wild straw splash
silk spools for your ears.
But where white spouts out spills

on your brow to clear
eyepools wheel shafts of light
R
o
s
e you are B
     l
     u
     e.

LOVE IS

a rain of diamonds
in the mind

the soul's fruit
sliced in two

a dark spring
loosed at the lips of light

under-earth waters
unlocked from their lurking
to sparkle in a crevice
parted by the sun

a temple
not of stone but cloud
beyond the heart's roar
and all violence

outside the anvil-stunned domain
unfrenzied space

between the grains of change
blue permanence

one short step
to the good ground

the bite into bread again

Dark wild honey, the lion's
eye color, you brought home
from a country store.
Tastes of the work of shaggy
bees on strong weeds,
their midsummer bloom.
My brain's electric circuit
glows, like the lion's iris
that, concentrated, vibrates
while seeming not to move.
Thick transparent amber
you brought home,
the sweet that burns.

Heat of the sun on wood of the deck. Spread flat,
my body accommodates to hardness on the worn boards.
Cat fools with my foot, trying to make my big toe
stay in her ear. She gets bored when you're not here.

House feels hollow, without vibration, asleep.
No sudden bumps or door-slams, no shuffled dishes,
no water rushing in the tub, or outside from the hose.
Vacuum's snarling inhale, hedge clipper's chatter —
any welcome racket would make the little cat leap up,

land four-footed like a springbok, and race downstairs
to see what you are making happen. Instead, all is
neat and peaceful. Phone never rings. Or, if it does,
receiver waits long to be raised.

If you were here, I wouldn't be this flat, sunbathing
a whole morning on the deck, half hearing the far
gargle of a helicopter over the bay. I get lazy when
you're away. I have to feel guilty that I don't do
all the Things To Do on today's list.

Whether I ought, or not, I'm blaming it on you
that kitten doesn't spring. Slow, from inside, wags
the old Seth Thomas pendulum. And from below I hear
the suspended slaps of the tide.

Kitten has quit fooling with my toe. She's collapsed
in the shade under the overhang, her blond belly-frill
barely moving with her breath, heavy little bucket-head
dropped on paws. The crossed blue eyes are shut.

To confirm a Thing and give thanks
               to the stars that named me
and fixed me in the Wheel of heaven
         my fate pricked out in the Boxer's chest
in the hips curled over the Horse
           Though girled in an apple-pink month
and the moon hornless
            the Brothers glitter in my wristbones
At ankle and knee I am set astride
               and made stubborn in love

In the equal Night where oracular beasts
                the planets depose
and our Selves assume their orbits
     I am flung where the Girdle's double studs
grant my destiny
             I am the Athletes in that zone
My thighs made marble-hard
           uncouple only to the Archer
with his diametrical bow
            who prances in the South
himself a part of his horse
       His gemmed arrow splits the hugging twins

The moon was gelded on that other night as well
         O his feeble kingdom we will tip over
If our feet traverse the milky way
   the earth's eccentric bead on which we balance
is small enough to hide between our toes
           its moon a mote that the Long Eye
is hardly conscious of
              nor need we be
The tough the sensuous Body our belief
        and fitting the pranks of Zeus

to this our universe
>we are Swans or Bulls as the music turns us
We are Children incorrigible and perverse
>>who hold our obstinate seats
on heaven's carousel
>>refusing our earth's assignment
refusing to descend
>>to beget such trifles of ourselves
as the gibbous Mothers do
>>We play in the Den of the Gods
and snort at death

Then let me by these signs
>>maintain my magnitude
as the candid Centaur his dynasty upholds
>>And in the Ecliptic Year
our sweet rebellions
>>shall not be occulted but remain
coronals in heaven's Wheel

On the Cliff

I'm sawing a slice off that hard dark knobby loaf
from Zabar's — black molasses and raisins in it —
to have with Tilsit cheese. You left a pumpkin and
autumn leaves on the stripped wood table, you filled
the birdfeeder hanging from the eaves. The window
is clean, the sill is varnished, white impatiens
in a brick clay pot smile above the sink. Our terrace
lined with boulders, the slate path with pachysandra
you planted. Storm doors are on, in front and back,
it's snug in here. I'm chewing, looking at the shelves
you cut and hung to hold our books and decoys.
You're strong, you twist off the lids of jars.
Cold nights you're a stove in bed.

By the Canal

For Valentine's Day a whole studio and library!
Shelves built to the ceiling, there's space for every
thing: papers, folders, files and books, books, books.
Binoculars and chess set, tape recorders, tapes and
jigsaw. Telephone that's a blue car has a shelf
of its own. The old maple sawhorse table fits right in
and looks brand new. Curly ivy on the sill and outside
an entire alphabet of birds, on the porch, in the yard.
You put pink ribbons of sunrise in the back window,
scarlet bands of sunset in the front, the moon above our
bed at night. It snowed. You made a path. The Christmas
poinsettia blooms all year.

I'm coming toward you
always
instep on the quivering wire
leaning aside
but never looking down
eyes unsmiling
immune to sleep
or hazard

I'm coming toward you

Always your pallid image leaps
behind the bars of distance
where merge sea and sky

Not setting with the sun
nor waning with the moon
your torso centaur-like
is prancing
upon my mind's rim

Fiercely taking aim
my body is a sharpened dart
of longing
coming toward you always

I lay my head on Love's breast and heard
the inconspicuous winepress of the blood
that labyrinths its body, its threads
rayed in cunning runnels from their source,
and heard the plushy piston with its push
replenish the murmurous vineyard of that flesh
that drinks perpetually its own
mystic grapes and breathes
the passion manufactured with its breath.

And I became so drenched and transfused
rising and falling on the breast of Love,
listening to its lever and inhaling
its distillation, heated and sweet,
that I a willing Bacchus became
who lived on laughter only, and
the brandy of sleep. Or else I was the twin of
Eros with most natural wings
soaring over fictions of necessity—

indecent, delicious, possessionless, except
for those ruthless accurate things
fated to fix love to youth, and sharp
arrest the heart. I became Love, so used
its fruits and instruments.
Arrest the heart? Oh, I am sure
it works still; its works are still
steady, salubrious, and a sanguine miracle.
I hear the soft and metric stamp,

the juice expelled but the juice contained, deployed
to invade the ruby ditches of desire.
Though we recline now on the long couch
as if enchanted, or awaiting incarnation,
and in sleep seem chiseled into legend,

it is I who wince touching a wound
(that is closed, and but a seam of stone),
I who feel the pincers of the wreath
and find my wrists and feet horrified

by holes, by omens I wish not to own.
I wish not to own Love's wine
in its flow may flow from a rift
and, siphoned outside the keep of the intact god,
stain and overflow a cannibal's lips—
crude, needy, feeding on love's hoot   the bleeding
called blessing—goblets filled from leaks
never healed, and faucets made of the hurts—
such a drunkard's bath furnished incessantly

that rips into flood, to inundate and swamp the heart.
These damages prefigured have sobered me.
I lie on the body of Love, listening, and I
feel its breast's fountain vivify
my veins. I warm to wake it again, that it may wake
me to feasts and battles, voyages, homecomings.
Though I know not its new form forming while it wakes,
but know the power it bears, changeless and endless.
And what thirsts it slakes in me.

I consecrate Love's body to delight
like that of the tree before Eden, when the trunk was white
and it wore no fruit. Oh, it is not
a backward twining through vines of regret,
or an ignorance of history's hardening and time's sly
depletion. But it is a stripping of the breast
of love—and if it must, let it be cursed
again—but may it wake
naked to instinct, as at first.

THE KISS

The thing itself is odd
this nibbled touching

contiguous thresholds
for the souls to pass
from porch to porch

Each a pod
snugly shut
wishes to open then divide
and so beget a sibling

To match as mittens do
identical and different

Master and mistress each
Then will I *be* you and bee you

In membranes locked
a peach and peach
would sip each other

Why this shock?
Ignition makes of parallels a peak
of straights a sphere

Heads together here
two rocks
the same space-pocket fills

Impossible such occupation
yet your face is mine
I stand behind your eyes

But then apart (a part) again
like boxers in ballet
The silken gloves
have barely grazed

The flick
of the immediate vanishes
Coincidence is quick

Before it tarnishes
O realize the truth of Two
the I the also You

AT FIRST, AT LAST

At first the dips are shallow,
the peaks ever higher.
Until at last the peaks

are lower.
The valleys deepen.
It is a wave

that mounts and recoils.
Coming then to shadows
on the slopes,

rifts in the concaves,
what is there to do
but lie open-eyed and love

the wave? The wave that gave us
high joys
never again to be matched,

and shall give us,
till it breaks,
oh what

surprises, releases, abysses?
To feel, to feel.
To be the implement

and the wound of feeling.
To lie open to feeling
on the exploding breast, the wave.

Lie still and let me love you
first with my eyes
that feast upon you
as on deep skies
to count the constellations
Below your breast Andromeda
Orion and the rest

Lie still and let me love you
now with my hands
that dream over your body
as in wondrous lands
skiers ascend sun-mantled peaks
and sweep to snow-smooth hollows
where silence speaks

Lie still and let me love you
with my mouth
pressed among strange flowers
elixirs of the south
to drink their dewy musk
or like rich grapes
I nuzzle with my lips
until their wine escapes

Lie still and let me love you
with all my weight
urgent upon you
Deep-keeled elate
my body greets you a leaping boat
challenging your tide
to be the stronger
And now afloat
lie still no longer

Demand I love you
the more the more
while passion's breakers
bear us to their shore

Life in the throat of my love leaps
though love is sleeping
under the eyelids of my love Look
a dream is darting
as the blood darts in the throat's vein
and love's shoulder warms my cheek
a dream floats to my love's brain

Heart in the chest of my love moves
though sleeping proving
the flesh of love will wake See
a breath is taken
as a dream makes the brow of my love smile
and the face's flower and the hair's leaves
quiver in a wind of love on that isle

where the heart beats now Watch
I will watch for the meeting
of my love with love in the heat
of the dream's full quaking
as love's body wakes in my arms' catch
and life in my chest and throat leaps
though love is sleeping

CODA TO J.

We lie together
dark and light
you asleep and I awake
our pulses oven-paced
our limbs interlocked
so familiar that on
your ledge of dream
you cannot tell my body
from your own

With me into the stream
I take your hand upon my thigh
our breathing keeps us tandem

While you sip
at the sable teat
I sail to a
light-filled tent
to a legendary wood
to a labyrinth
to find your image
where it first stood

Who are you I saw running
down streets of dream
with long stride running aloofly
breasting the milky dawn
stepping upon your shadow
and leaving no footprint?

When you had run far down
that path and made exit
into the corner of distance
I awoke with your image in my eye
barely as tall as my pupil

Since then I have looked
for you in every street
gazed down each vague avenue
run headlong many nights
to strange horizons
and panting have returned
not finding you

You are in one of those
towns and dawn is on the cobbles
not so far from here
around this corner

You are in one of those
stealthy towns of sleep
running in the street
stepping upon your shadow
leaving no footprint

WE ARISE FROM THE PIT OF NIGHT

When we return to the cool daylight
where ships of words slacken
no longer burn
instead are silken bandages for pain
the rigid rack where we have lain
become a cushion kinder than snow
our breasts unite and we forget
the murders sunken there below

We lie curled like children
in smooth-limbed innocence
but for night's stigma on our eyelids
The bruised corpses hurled
into the unconscious cave
have swept our minds bare
Caresses still can save us
from their stare

Is there an hour inching toward us
containing the final effigy
of love which we will slay
the last volt of our power
to check it spent?
Will we then in horror unalloyed
confront each other with a void
from which no sprig of pity
no green leaf of grief will spring
no living thing
which only the black well of hate
will inundate?

Sleep wash us clean
Sun charge our flesh with radiance
Make us pure
as when in the green beginning
we trusted one another
Love veil our pupils as before

BEAST

my Brown self
goes on four paws
supple-twining in the
lewd Gloom

arching against the
shaggy hedges
with a relishing Purr
tasting among his
spurted fur

the Ripeness
brisk and willing
of his brown body

yawning Obscurely
glittered-glancing
couching himself
in the sunny places

beating his tail
where traces
of She-odor make
a pattern for
his unbrained thought

feeling the Budding
thorns in his
feet of felt

planning to Stab them
into the wincing pelt
of a creature smaller

my Brown self
a thing gleam-jawed
goes downright
Four-pawed

My eyes
flicker over you
like flames
to lick you up

are cooled
by your beauty

blue loops
ripple you
like tongue-tips

furling with
the serpents
of your thighs

into the whorl
of your haunches
and the slender trap
of your waist

gliding the
gulled column
of your back

your neck and head
its ornament

over your
belly's plateau
flat and palpitant

to your breasts
which are
perched birds
plump and alert

their little beaks
sharply lifted

You stand in Egyptian
stillness
accomplished
calm as bronze

and the fuses
of my veins
fill with quickfire

I've got what I want
Nakedness   The sky
pouring blue in my eye
Downy just-born clouds
to dive between
The virility of the sun

Time's Book does not turn
its pages   The world
is arranged as I left it
Past and future on either side
Its work is being done

Page 199 on my left hand
hidden   My love goes to
office in the city
Page 1099 on my right
hand hidden   Affronted
by old age I commit suicide

Time's Book is open
to the middle   Its pages
are mirrors for cool clouds
The naked swimmer
turns gold in the font
of the sun   Erased is pity
and dreadful truth
Unchanged and wide
warm windless without harm
the present and my youth

Is there anything I want?
Yes   My love to be here
to love me   Are there

other people in Time's Book?
Other events   Soldiers
dying   Women in childbirth?

Of course   But I have
arranged them to be
as they are

A clearing her forehead. Brisk wilderness
of hair retreats from the smooth dancing ground,
now savage drums are silent. In caves of shade
twin jaguars couch, flicking their tails
in restless dream. Awake they leap in unison,
asleep they sink like embers.
Sloping swards her cheekbones graduate to
a natural throne. Two lambs her nostrils curled
back-to-back. Follow the shallow hollow to
her lip-points, stung blossoms or bruised fruits,
her lower lip an opulent orchard, her spiral smile
a sweet oasis both hot and cool.
Soft in center, swollen, a bole of moss
hiding white stones and a moist spring
where lives a snake so beautiful and shy,
his undulant hole is kept a slippery secret.
A cleft between the cliff-edge and her mouth,
we drop to the shouldered foothills down the neck's
obelisk, and rest. In the valley's scoop
velvet meadowland.

DAFFODILDO

A daffodil from Emily's lot
I lay beside her headstone
on the first day of May.
I brought
another with me, threaded
through my buttonhole, the spawn
of ancestor she planted
where, today,
I trod her lawn.
A yellow small decanter
of her perfume, hermit-wild
and without a stopper,
next to her stone I filed
to give her back her property —
it's well it cannot spill.
Lolling on my jacket,
Emily's other daffodil.

Now, rocking to the racket
of the train, I try
recalling all her parlor's
penetration of my eye,
remembering mainly spartan
sunlight through the dimity
of the window-bay, evoking
her white-dressed anonymity.
I remember, as if spoken
in my head: "I'm
nobody! Who
are you?"
thinking
how liked by time
she still is. It has linked
the hemlocks closer in their

hedge so that her privacy
remains. A denser lair,
in fact, than when she was alive
and looked through that bay
on the long garden
where I looked today.

  Another lady is its warden
now. She smells like bread
and butter. A New England pug-
face, she's eighty-seven, may be dead
before another host of plugless
yellow daintycups
springs next spring in the grass.
(What if one white bulb still sups
sun-time that Emily's shoe passed
over?) That old
black-dressed lady told
me, "Here's where
she soaked her gowns in this square
copper boiler on hot bricks." Whiteness
takes much washing. "Oh, her chair,"
she said, suddenly sprightly,
leading me up the stair
to a blue bedroom. "Mustn't forget to
show you
that. It's stored
in a closet." She brought out
a seat for a four-
year-old, only the cane devoutly
replaced, the ladderback and
legs of cherrywood original.
"An awe came on the trinket,"
one article her hand

would have known all
its life.

    "Geneva's farthest skill,"
I pondered,
"can't put the puppet
bowing," and retrieved
an answer,
    "I dwell
in Possibility—
a fairer
house than Prose." Yellow
bells in the still
air of their green room
out there
under the upstairs window
mutely swung.
    Shining through their cups,
her sunny ghost
passed down the rows.
"A word is dead
when it is said,
some say.
I say
it just begins to live that day."

    To her headstone I walked uphill.
It stands white without arrogance
on a green plot
that is her myth-filled
lot
now. Almost blank. Relatives
shoulder her in a straight rank.
Emily, 130 years older

since you took your
little throne
when you were four,
I crane
but can never
gain
that high chair
where you will ever
sit! Alone.

Self-confessed, and rocking
to the racket of the train,
I play back how
I picked you for my pocket,
stooped at your plain
stone.
    One gold dildo
I leave you from the host
I stole;
the other, holy,
I will keep until
it shrinks to ghost.
    "Disdaining men,
and oxygen,"
your grassy
breast I kiss
and make
this vow, Emily, to "take
vaster
attitudes—and strut upon my stem."

Most of what is happening is hidden.
There is a subworld
where the roots of things exist.
You happen to say a few words
along with a sudden smile.
The first hyacinth unfurls
on an April morning: color, odor,
texture complete, and in plain sight.
Below that bright floor a crepuscular
network, the depth and spread of thought
takes up great space,
and travels. The roots are ramifying,
counterpart to a sprig of brief perfume.
A huge and delicate tree, inverted there
in the nether dark. A crop of dense hair
feels downward, outward, to draw up
the sustaining sap.

SOMEBODY WHO'S SOMEBODY

(Draft, never finished; title supplied)

Somebody who's somebody
    often doesn't look like somebody
until you look
    inside.
Elizabeth's liver is tattooed
    with the intaglio of an indigo turtle.
Not emblazoned—
    that would augur prominence
and a definite who's who-ness
    No—nobodyness is the ultimate
achievement achieved
    secretly, invisibly but indelibly
inside.

(O but remember, E,
    I saw you pee on the floor
at Yaddo long ago)
    Enviable that ennoblement
that accrues from the peasant's
    modest and unmodish stance,
the man with the hoe (that's really
    a scepter *inside*),
the low brow that hides
    a hemisphere heapish as a hive.
O golden bees of your eccentric
    thinkishness, each a queen hermited
within—the hairdo like mud
    round the armature of cobwebs,
but mansioned behind that seedy
    façade what a Midas realm,
what orderly glitter, your honey
    mausoleum private
and impenetrable, perfectly
    coned and sealed except for the little

arched bunghole where over the draw-
     bridge of your tongue the worker words
pass forth.

But E, remember
     we tried to find Lake Lonely long ago
wandering awkwardly beside
     the yellow reeds, the ditch-black
waters, and played at darts
     in the Paddock Bar by the racetrack.
You read my "Lion" and
     I your "Little Exercise."
You got drunk and snickered, air
     whistled through your teeth at
dinner, everyone thought you were
     silly. I burned from head to foot
for you, hoping they hadn't
     noticed. Later you peed on
the floor—just a drop or two—at
     West House— because the
bathroom was locked. I felt
     responsible—I should have had
a toilet in my pocket, to produce
     in the moment of your
unpostponable need. I was nuts
     about you. And I couldn't say
a word. And you never said *the*
     word that would have loosened
all my doggy love and let me
     jump you like a suddenly
unhobbled hound wild for love.

Little Elizabeth
     who still keeps me

wild at the end of your chain—because
    I can't reach you, have never
pawed you, slaver at the thought
    of you still, because because
I have never *known* you years
    and years—and love
the unknown you.

LAOCOÖN DREAM RECORDED IN DIARY
DATED 1943

In half-sleep I felt an arm go round me,
but longer than an arm, it lapped me twice
and I was bound, but did not mind.
One supple coil lay nice about my waist
without alarm and, skilled and strong,
the other winding cool and careful, slipped
to my hip, tightening without haste.
An odd thrill made a geyser in my blood.
This love had a new taste.

Now the arms were three, all slick
along my nakedness, and thick.
A fourth, more slender, hugged my thigh.
I did not wake. Dream-submerged
as in a tepid lake, I lay, postponing fear.
A quick and tender tongue flicked at my neck,
groped higher, licked into my ear.
Below I felt each toe receive a velvet ring,
and soon there sat around my ankles
worm-wet bracelets, fat and glistening.

Cap-eyed, caressed all ways at once,
I did not care to identify my lover, nor dare
apprise him by a finger-try. My hands
crept to my head. A thousand tousled vipers
rippled there, from braid and curlicue
had made their lair. With lips of suede
they grazed upon my brows, breathed hissing
kisses to my mouth and, seething, sipped
my nipples, where mini-eels, each narrow
as a hair, sprouted in a copious stream.

Roused, I could not rise. Anger and desire
were one. A ton of horror poured an equal

weight of lust, of drowsy hate, of heavy
bliss like a drug upon my dream.
The five arms held me snug.
Roped by a riddle in spiral shape
in a lunar nightmare I was ready for rape.

A gentle murderer whose many-stranded will
never could be severed, nor a motive in the kill
unraveled, the six arms traveled me entire,
and trussed me heel to nape.
I, the victim recognizing all my strangled
cries at lies, my tangled fears as wishes
in disguise, snatched the seventh arm,
greater than the rest, with both my own
and pressed it close. Its wide girth
matched my chest. Its voracious face,
the jaws agape, avid on the vipers fed.
Into that hollow my head was swallowed, open-eyed.
The dream was done, so there was no escape.

A PAIR

A he
and she,
prowed upstream,
soot-brown
necks,
bills the green
of spring
asparagus,

heads
proud figure-
heads for the boat-
bodies, smooth
hulls on feathered   the two,
water,   browed with light,
                              steer ashore,
                                rise: four
                                    web-
                            paddles pigeon-
                                      toe it
                              to the reeds;

he
walks first,
proud, prowed
as when light-
browed, swimming,
he leads.

Creases in his clothes
creases in his flesh
creases in his arteries
The inner walls shrinking
while the outer walls slip and shift flabbily
Pepper grains in the chin-furrows
in the pale ear-basins
the inelastic lobes sagging tits

She sits still
until it is over
holding her breath her tongue curled back
like a fastidious animal
aloof before an old cur
circling and sniffing her

The bald unfevered brow
the eyes anaemic fish
each under a goldrimmed glass dish
fish suffocating on sand
rills of watery blood in their scales
suddenly pressed between the thrusts of her breast

His hands with wormy veins
tremble tentatively climbing her arms
tightening to the round bare bicep
his nails rasp on silk

His palms feel like old cold rubber
but she does not shudder
it is too ludicrous for that

I'm not going to hurt you
Of course he's not
Who could be hurt but him

Juiceless chameleon
dragging his belly through clover
Detected at once he is crunched
by his own steel heel of self-esteem

If I were younger What's the use
I'm older still I reek
against her so-green cheek
And there between beneath
it flips and flaps like a hen's dewlaps
but the stem bends will not swell with its lust
The very breath in my chest
the blood of the pump alloyed
with dust and rust

When we are young the wizard's wand
waves in vain
above our dumb and glossy flesh
though we could use it then
had we the palate precious and fresh
When we are sunken diminished stale
it sometimes seems
(oh memories of embraces
not as they felt but as they would now feel
now that the dams are closing
the torrent choked to a trickle)
that could we rub ourselves in roses
wallow in new-squeezed milk
our gray skin sloppy like a too-large suit
would tense and firm and fit us slim again
and we'd be keen as jack-knives
and arrogant again

His glazed tongue hunts
between her hard bud-lips

for the moisture of youth profuse
A draft of it would she let it flow to him
his last lascivious dregs
grimed with fear
(but for that the more rare)
would turn to sharp wine in his shrunken flask
Purple kiss like a plum
returned to him she would not miss
(the tree is so laden)
But too raw with spring she is
unwilling to admit ripeness
at least for him

She holds her breath waiting
until it is over

Over its cliff
splashes the
little rapids,
a braid of glossy
motion in perpetual
flow and toss,
its current rayed
flashing down
crayon veins.

Life-node of my
precipice of bone,
a snake-mouth muscle
spills urgent venom
to soft hills,
to flesh-warm stone.

A replica of all
power's crotched
here in the ribs,
knot and nubbin
of the jutting flood.
Leaps and drops
are instants in
the swirling hour
reiterated from
this hub:

Grief-gusher,
freshet of desire,
snug nest of joy
and fear,
its zest constant
even in sleep,

its padded roar
bounding in the
grotto of the breast.

Hinge of hate and
love, steep springhead,
riddle of my blood,
primal pool of
cruelty, and all
queer sweet thrills . . .
Ravine of my body,
red, incredulous
with autumn,
from here curt death
will hurl me delirious
into the gorge.

THIS IS WHAT MY LOVE IS THINKING

His meekness is more terrible than any vice

Amity makes for contentment
but violence is creation

I am chained by the chains which I have fastened
on him

I do not dare to tire of him before he shall have
tired of me

and if this happened
I should be even more obliged to stay bound

I could break with him utterly
if I thought he would weep

but he would hide his pain
thus forcing me to condemn myself

If only he would do that
which would make me hate him

but then, not to match his meanness
I would have to forgive him
and so tighten the knot

Still I do not want to be rid of him
I only want to be free

To possess myself only
and so be lonely?
Or to lose myself wholly
to win what can never be mine
solely?

My hands are murder-red. Many a plump head
drops on the heap in the basket. Or, ripe
to bursting, they might be hearts, matching
the blackbird's wing-fleck. Gripped to a reed
he shrieks his ko-ka-ree in the next field.
He's left his peck in some juicy cheeks, when
at first blush and mostly white, they showed
streaks of sweetness to the marauder.

We're picking near the shore, the morning
sunny, a slight wind moving rough-veined leaves
our hands rumple among. Fingers find by feel
the ready fruit in clusters. Here and there,
their squishy wounds . . . Flesh was perfect
yesterday . . . June was for gorging . . .
sweet hearts young and firm before decay.

"Take only the biggest, and not too ripe,"
a mother calls to her girl and boy, barefoot
in the furrows. "Don't step on any. Don't
change rows. Don't eat too many." Mesmerized
by the largesse, the children squat and pull
and pick handfuls of rich scarlets, half
for the baskets, half for avid mouths.
Soon, whole faces are stained.

A crop this thick begs for plunder. Ripeness
wants to be ravished, as udders of cows when hard,
the blue-veined bags distended, ache to be stripped.
Hunkered in mud between the rows, sun burning
the backs of our necks, we grope for, and rip loose
soft nippled heads. If they bleed—too soft—
let them stay. Let them rot in the heat.

When, hidden away in a damp hollow under moldy
leaves, I come upon a clump of heart-shapes
once red, now spiderspit-gray, intact but empty,
still attached to their dead stems —
families smothered as at Pompeii — I rise
and stretch. I eat one more big ripe lopped
head. Red-handed, I leave the field.

I wander out, the lone pedestrian
in Lafayette, and walk the west
side of the Wabash past the Sunday
houses. Don't know where you are,
hope *not* to meet you—but
you're snowing in my mind. "About
that telegram you sent: I thought
the initials meant from Bobby K.
Wired back 'Thank you.' They
typed it 'Fuck you,' and now he's
sore at me. See how you screw up
all the time—though with the best
intentions?" You laugh, and I
congratulate myself: "The Smothers
Brothers ought to get me to write
their gags." I see you pull
the word-strips off like sunburned
skin, standing in your ski coat in
my living room—you couldn't get it
off, the zipper was jammed—I didn't
offer to help. I had a toothache,
and here you'd come, a day early and
without phoning first, butting at
my door. You walk, head down, like
a sun-stunned bull, did you know?
You left the Volks as usual turned on
at the curb, shoved a bag of Key limes
at me, *pretending* you weren't coming
in, when you knew damn well I'd
invite you—would *have* to, wouldn't I?
to feel—to feel the human in you—
to love it—love your *self*, first,
foremost—let your body take care—
of you in it—the you that loves.

I almost called that cop named King
you know. Took his number along to
the movie Friday, just in case.
You're ugly when angry, Nasty Mouth.
Angry when sick, I know—but sick
because self-beaten, bruised, starved,
strafed, driven on, tired out, shot
down. Snow's deep blue now. Twilight
out the window. It's Sunday night.
"In this nook that opens south..."
was Wednesday you came   I'd
started to write—and brought me limes.
When I wouldn't play the game the way,
somewhere in your head since Florida,
you thought I would, and ought—that
head that cannot dream if, as you say,
it never sleeps—"The head is dead..."
No, that was then—a summer time,
in "Good day, sunshine" weather-blond
head, dazzled grin, on the snapshot
you labeled your "2nd happiest day"—
and I was supposed to say, "What is
the first?"—and didn't, since supposed
to. That head—Goldy Lox—with foolish red cap
on— you holding my foot instead of
hand that night I had toothache—
expecting to make me, weren't you?—
"I can get anyone in the world
interested in me"—You told on
yourself there, you know—and all
that you told about getting dumped
in front of the Waldorf—about faking
it out in the interview at Rutgers—
about "Arne being used to it"—you
freaking out on him—"I'm a little

unreliable once in a while," you
admitted. "But notice my charm, my
cool—I do my dirt with style,"
your cocky chuckle said. You swiping
the air and pacing the rug. You told
on yourself there, Bouncer—over and
over—and when you bounced that
volleyball off the wall so's to barely
miss my head—"that hair" you crow
over and snow me about—"I thought
if I could touch it just one more
time." Before you climb the cliff, I'm
supposed to think. Can't you see you
kissed yourself off, slugged yourself
out, dumped on yourself all that
evening? Hauled away the record player,
threw down Webster's 3rd in its place,
on the bed, like a slab of ice. Christ,
you're funny! Wish I could laugh,
like I used to, two months back. You
made me glad then—crazy glad—
unleashed, MacLeished, I believed you—
Like I said, "I believe everything you
say till I find out different." Well,
I've found out, haven't I? You aced
yourself right out of the game, and
just when it was ripe, you thought, to
run all your way. You've got big cards
—so big you throw them away. I had
my little significant present for you—
Had you got it in N.Y. from R., would
all of it now be different, I wonder?
Maybe, and maybe worse. We might be
that gun you've got between us—me

wasting more of my time than I'm
doing now, with this not-poem, trying
to plough you out of my mind. Snow's
falling on all the squirrels in all
the heavy arms of all the pines out
there, where it's dark. It's yellow
in here. Goldy, you wouldn't take my
gold-wrapped trinket—and I had
Russian Leather for you, too—to make
you—smell so good—And you threw
back my mother's 25-carat gold ring
along with a nasty misspelled note
making those funny *d*'s that you do—
And you threw me gold yarn sox you'd
knitted—that makes 4 pair—with the
mistake you warned me was in one toe—
And threw me 2 basketball tickets clipped
to a sweet note next morning, Thursday,
in my mailbox. Then phoned. I was
still asleep. "Can you give me
breakfast?" I said, "No"—and didn't
thank you for anything—stayed mute
and mum—disconnected—But this was
before I'd been to the mailbox, remember?
You so demanding, so damned awake and
breathless. My tooth hurt, I wasn't up
yet—said "Call me later." You snarled:
"*You* call *me*." So I didn't. OK, so
somehow—but how?—how should I know, with
you it was more than a sore tooth?
And after the dentist, and after I'd
been working all day on that mistake-of-
a-piece for the mag for you—you
dumbbunny, diddling with that sycophant

dumbdaddy A., who you say you've thrown
over because you dropped a critical
stitch back there somewhere, made a booboo
with the manipulation switch—and had
it about done and off my neck so I could
think about starting to do what I had
been supposed to do, *my* work, all day—
No, wait a minute, that was the *next*
day, Friday—Thursday I made you take
me to the lecture, but you were late, and
I walked and met you in the Volks—you
were dolled up, net stockings on, band-
aids showing through where you'd banged
yourself on the squash court—By the
way, Tony that night—No, that had to
be Friday—Anyway, he limped, I can
tell you that—You strained a muscle
in his buttock—he could hardly walk
upstairs. I'm laughing now. I'm
laughing! It feels good. Bouncer,
you idiot, you Wild Thing—it's you,
you know, they sing about in Bobby's
voice on the top ten—"With those
initials you could be President."
"I'm gonna be a big man in town..."
"I'm gonna make it..." I've got you
humming that. I liked the back
of your bully neck in my hand—I
can't stand it if I've been too
mean to you—Have I been? I didn't
mean to. You—last time I saw you,
at the lecture—nodded you out—
and showed how you'd learned one
lesson—you didn't fade, until I

told you that line, did you?—with my, I guess
you thought, disdainful nod. It
wasn't meant to be. I'm just lost—
more or less, like you. Only more—
scared—and hate myself for that.
And when I hate myself I go cold
and stiff, I settle in—into my
self, old horse in blankets armed—
or old stubborn horny turtle.
Remember how you said you shot
at them in the Keys? But didn't hit
any, you said. That's good. And you
are, too. But crazy. And I drive
you. To that. I know. That's why
you and I—can't. "Snowy gull and
sooty crow..." You see? It's late
now. I'm alone. And want to be.
Stopped snowing.

All yesterday was silent. Saturday.
There's more. There's lots more. Have
to stop now. I wish you well. Where
you are. Hear your voice on phone say:
"Good-bye, though." After I said, "I
hope you'll feel. Better." Those words,
if last, were gentle. Where did you
go? After you broke my door-
knob off? I want to, and I don't
want to, know.

Not the dress
not the skin
not the flesh.
Farther in.
Not the heart.
Then the beat?
The question steady
startles it.
Here the thread
here the knot:
Endure
by sway and rhythm
motion depending
on future's pause
Hear the plot.

BLEEDING

Stop bleeding said the knife.
I would if I could said the cut.
Stop bleeding you make me messy with this blood.
I'm sorry said the cut.
Stop or I will sink in farther said the knife.
Don't said the cut.
The knife did not say it couldn't help it but it sank in farther.
If only you didn't bleed said the knife I wouldn't have to do this.
I know said the cut I bleed too easily I hate that I can't
help it I wish I were a knife like you and didn't have to bleed.
Meanwhile stop bleeding will you said the knife.
Yes you are a mess and sinking in farther said the cut I will
have to stop.
Have you stopped by now said the knife.
I've almost stopped I think.
Why must you bleed in the first place said the knife.
For the reason maybe that you must do what you must do said the cut.
I can't stand bleeding said the knife and sank in farther.
I hate it too said the cut I know it isn't you it's me
you're lucky to be a knife you ought to be glad about that.
Too many cuts around said the knife they're mess I don't know
how they stand themselves.
They don't said the cut.
You're bleeding again.
No I've stopped said the cut. See you're coming out now the
blood is drying it will rub off you'll be shiny again and clean.
If only cuts wouldn't bleed so much said the knife coming out a little.
But then knives might become dull said the cut.
Aren't you bleeding a little said the knife.
I hope not said the cut.
I feel you are just a little.
Maybe just a little but I can stop now.
I feel a little wetness still said the knife sinking in
a little but then coming out a little.
Just a little maybe just enough said the cut.
That's enough now stop now do you feel better now said the knife.
I feel I have to bleed to feel I think said the cut.
I don't I don't have to feel said the knife drying now becoming shiny.

127

ZAMBESI AND RANEE

*Because their mothers refused to nurse them, the two
female animals in this compartment were reared together
by hand from early infancy. . . . They are firm friends and
strongly resent separation. While Zambesi, the lion, is
inclined to be rough and aggressive, Ranee, the tiger, easily
dominates her.*

—from a plaque at the Bronx Zoo

The tiger looks the younger and more male,
her body ribbed with staves as black as Bengal's
    in the next den. Clear green her eyes,
    in the great three-cornered head, set slantwise;
her hips as lean, her back as straight,
she's a velvet table when she walks, and able
      to bound ten feet to the level where her meat
      is flung at feeding time.

The lion, square-bodied, heavy-pelted, less grand,
her maneless, round-eared head held low,
    slouches and rocks in sand-colored nakedness,
    drag-bellied, watchful and slow; her yellow eyes
jealous, something morose in the down-hook
    of her jaw; her tail, balled at the end,
    like a riding crop taps at the bars.

They twine their shared pavilion, each spine
tracing an opposite figure eight. Paired females,
    they avoid each other's touch; but if, passing,
    as much as a whisker of that black-and-orange head
grazes the lion's flank, her topaz eye narrows:
    irascibly she turns with slugger's paw
    to rake the ear of her mate.

Then rampant, they wrestle; rich snarls
in coils pour from their throats and nostrils.
    Like soft boulders the bodies tumble each other down.
    And then, not bothering to rise, they lounge,

entangled chest to chest. Not hate embroils them,
but that neither will be humble to the other;
    nor will the tiger, in earnest, test her quickness
    against the lion's weight.

Few sights can still surprise us in the zoo,
    though this is the place for marvels.
These odd heroines do attract us. Why?
Crouched on sinewy elbows, sphinxes, they project
    vast boredom. Those still heads outstare
    some horizon of catlike time, while we, in vain,
expect a gleam from eye to eye between them,
a posture of affection, or some clue...

Bemused at the bars, some watchers smile and read
Zambesi and Ranee upon their card:
    They might ring the bell, introduce themselves
    and be welcome. The life these ladies lead,
upon a stage repeats itself behind the walls
    of many city streets; silent, or aloud,
    the knowing crowd snickers.

Refused to nurse them, simpering mothers read,
and tighten the hold on Darling's hand: "Look
    at the pussy cats!" they coax, they croon,
    but blushing outrage appalls their cheeks—
that this menage calls down no curse,
not only is excused, but celebrated.
    They'd prefer these captives punished, who
    appear to wear the brand some captivated humans do.

GOODNIGHT

He and the wind
She and the house

Slow from the house
whose mellow walls
have fondled him
slow from the
yellow threshold
to the purple wind

Harsh as a dog's tongue
the licking wind
upon her throat
Rough it wraps
and fondles her
as slow into the night
he walks

She and the house now only
He and the wind

Finally got the horse broke in. It took years.
Now, not strong enough to ride it. It was wild,
and ornery, yes. Which came, in part, from its not
knowing it was a horse, meant to be ridden.
Wouldn't look you in the eye. Shied from looking
itself in the eye. Wouldn't look in the mirror,
especially not in back. Didn't know it *had* a back.
Funny, how it followed. Didn't have to be caught.
It offered its back, asked for the saddle. Or, so
I thought. A joke! Throw you? That
horse wouldn't let you touch lip or nose with your
feeding hand, let alone get a leg over. Yet it hung
around, acting as if. Acting as if. Would come up
behind you, nuzzle your neck. You'd turn, grab
for its mane. It slid away. But never kept
away for long. Unpredictable. Drove you crazy.
Made you ornery. Broke *you*. Wish I was strong now,
and that horse not so strong. It wouldn't take long.
To have it. Gentled. Ready to mount. Eager to have
me. Eating out of its hand.

A NEW PAIR

Like stiff whipped cream in peaks and tufts afloat,
the two on barely gliding waves approach.

One's neck curves back, the whole head to the eyebrows
hides in the wing's whiteness.

The other drifts erect, one dark splayed foot
lifted along a snowy hull.

On thin, transparent platforms of the waves
the pair approach each other, as if without intent.

Do they touch? Does it only seem so to my eyes'
perspective where I stand on shore?

I wish them together, to become one fleece enfolded, proud
vessel of cloud, shape until now unknown.

Tense, I stare and wait, while slow waves carry them
closer. And side does graze creamy side.

One tall neck dips, is laid along the other's back,
at the place where an arm would embrace.

A brief caress. Then both sinuous necks arise,
their paddle feet fall to water. As I stare,
with independent purpose at full sail, they steer apart.

THE REST OF MY LIFE

Sleeping Alone

Waiting for first light,
for the lift of the curtain,
for the world to ripen,
tumbling toward the sun,

I lie on my side,
head sunk in the pillow,
legs upfolded,
as if for Indian burial.

My arms are friends
relaxed beside each other.
One hand, open, touches,
brings warmth to the other.

A Spring Morning

Your right hand and my left
hand, as if they were bodies
fitting together, face each other.

As if we were dancing. But
we are in bed. The thumb of your
hand touches my cheek. My head

feels the cool of the pillow.
Your profile, eye and ear and lip
asleep, has already gone

through the doorway of your dream.
The round-faced clock ticks on,
on the shelf in dawnlight.

Your hand has met mine,
but doesn't feel my cheek is wet.
From the top of the oak

outside the window, the oriole
over and over repeats its
phrase, a question.

Unable to Write It

Tears do not make good ink.
Their message invisible,
no one reads this hurt.

I lie alone in dirt despair.
Alone beside one who does not feel
lightning strike and agony crackle.

I sink into black, the inkwell
wordless, filled with tears.

What Matters

It may be that it doesn't matter
who or what or why you love.
(Maybe it matters when, and for how long.)
Of course, what matters is how strong.

Maybe the forbidden, the unbelievable,
or what doesn't respond—
what grabs all and gives nothing—
what is ghoul or ghost,
what proves you a fool,

shrinks you, shortens your life,
if you love it, *it* doesn't matter.
Only the love matters—
the stubbornness, or the helplessness.

At a certain chemical instant
in early youth, love's trigger is cocked.
Whatever moves into focus
behind the cross hairs, magnifies,
is marked for target, injected with
magic shot. But the target doesn't matter

The Rest of My Life

I'm the one
who'll be with me
for the rest of my life.

I'm the one
who'll enjoy myself,
take care of myself,
be lovable, so as to love
myself for the rest
of my life.

Arms, be strong to hold me.
Eyes, be with me.
Will you be with me
for the rest of my life?

I'm the one,
the only one,
the one who won't leave me
for the rest of my life.

I'm One

I do not have.
I do not expect.
I do not owe.

I'm one,
the only one,
free in my life.

Each day perfect,
each day a thousand years.
Time is in me.

I swallow the sun.
I'm the one, the only
one in my life.

Oh, windless day
within me,
Oh, silence and sun.

DIGGING IN THE GARDEN OF AGE
I UNCOVER A LIVE ROOT

For E.W.

The smell of wet geraniums. On furry
leaves, transparent drops rounded
as cats' eyes seen sideways.
Smell of the dark earth, and damp
brick of the pots you held, tamped empty.
Flash of the new trowel. Your eyes
green in greenhouse light. Smell of
your cotton smock, of your neck
in the freckled shade of your hair.
A gleam of sweat in your lip's scoop.
Pungent geranium leaves, their wet
smell when our widening pupils met.

I show her how to put her arms around me,
but she's much too small.
What's worse, she doesn't understand.
And
although she lies beside me, sticking
out her tongue, it's herself she licks.

She likes my stroking hand.
And
even lets me kiss.
But at my demand:
"Now, do it to me, like this,"
she backs off with a hiss.

What's in her little mind?
Jumping off the bed,
she shows me her behind,
but curls up on the rug instead.
I beg her to return. At first, she did,
then went and hid

under the covers. She's playing with my feet!
"Oh, Boa, come back. Be sweet.
Lie against me here when I'm nice and warm.
Settle down. Don't claw, don't bite.
Stay with me tonight."
Seeming to consent, she gives a little whine.

Her deep, deep pupils meet mine
with a look that holds a flood . . .
But not my brand.
Not at all.
And,
what's worse, she's much too small.

THE RED BIRD TAPESTRY

Now I put on the thimble of dream
    to stitch among leaves the red node of his body
and fasten here the few beads of his song.

Of the tree a cage of gilded spines
    to palace his scarlet, cathedral his cry,
and a ripple from his beak I sew,
    a banner bearing seven studs,
this scarf to be the morning that received his stain.

I do with thought instead of actuality
    for it has flown.
With glinting thimble I pull back, pull back
    that freak of scarlet to his throne:

To worship him, enchanted cherry to a tree
    that never bore such fruit—
who tore the veil of possibility
    and swung here for a day,
a never-colored bird, a never-music heard,
    who, doubly wanded then, looped away.

To find, in hollow of my throat, his call,
    and try his note on all the flutes of memory,
until that clear jet rinses me
    that was his single play—
for this I wear his daring and his royal eye.

Now perfected, arrested in absence—
    my needle laid by and spread my hand—
his claws on stems of my fingers fastened,
    rooted my feet and green my brow,
I drink from his beak the seven beads dropping:
    I am the cage that flatters him now.

ASLEEP

His shadowed face is closed   His eyes
are turned backward and down
His body lies without to guard the gate
of the mind's town   Sinking he has
for tether a braid of breath   Time
suspends the diver who plays with death

Trusting the tide he willingly returns
to a lost island in a nameless sea
as a dog unleashed leaps headlong
to the wind on the
unconscious scent of memory   His body lies behind
upon the shore   The salty flood rises
and murmurs in his blood

INCANTATION

Bright sleep bathing breathing walking
snow ocean and fire
spinning white and flinching green
red-and-yellow-petaled sheen
color me with fresh desire

Vast sleep snow as deep
fresh the leap to green and steep flinching wave
pulsing red glowers flow on black below

In black sleep brightness keep
in colored day spin and play
fresh foam sharp snow the slime of time whirl away
Fire is air is breath and green
lakes of air I walking swim

Powers are of motion made
of color braided all desire
In red and yellow flowers bathe
in snow ocean and fire
in snowy sleep on curls of flame
on shingles of the sea I climb
Dim and gray whirl away and knotted thought and slime

Burning snow spin me so with black sea
to braided be   In green sleep eons leap
from gray slime past thought and time
to pith and power to bathe in the immortal hour
to breathe from another pulsing flower

Snow ocean white fire
color me with fresh desire

Pebbles by their shadows
on sand in the slant
light look transparent.
Hollows bare feet stamped
fill up with blue shade.
Water with granular
yearning hones the whetstone
of the bank. A panting
wind begins, fresh and rank,
like the smell of love.

SAY YOU LOVE

Say you love
and do not be afraid
when that word comes singly
to your ear
a gift too rare
will in surrender fade

Let in its thousand echoes
without fear

Love's source is lavish
as the sun
Not in special veins
its juices run
Never expended
the molten store clots
quickens and
flowing becomes more
replenishing all things
in varied range

Then do not doubt love's substance
in its change

Take love
in full belief
and let it go
unclenched when it has warmed you
with its glow

Give love
as guiltless clouds
release their rain
to thirsty grass
that it may spring again

INDEX

May Swenson kept a master index in which she noted publication information as well as the date she began each poem. Those dates follow the poems listed here. In the absence of a beginning date, the publication date is given.

ABOUT THE POET

May Swenson was born on May 28, 1913, in Logan, Utah, and died on December 4, 1989, in Ocean View, Delaware. In that lifetime she worked as a newspaper reporter, ghostwriter, editor, secretary, manuscript reader for New Directions, and poet in residence, but always and mainly as a poet. Eleven volumes of her poetry were published during her lifetime. These earned her much praise from fellow poets, a place in the hearts and minds of poetry lovers, and many awards, among them the Brandeis University Creative Arts Award; Rockefeller, Guggenheim, and Ford fellowships; the Bollingen Prize for Poetry; a grant from the National Endowment for the Arts; an honorary doctor of letters degree from Utah State University; and a MacArthur fellowship. She was a member of the American Academy and Institute of Arts and Letters and a chancellor of the Academy of American Poets.